THE ADVENTURES OF AKANA

THE ANCESTRAL BEQUEST

by
Susan A. Ngong

All rights reserved. It is illegal to reproduce, duplicate or transmit any part of this book in either electronic means or printed format. Recording of this publication is strictly prohibited. No part of this publication may be reproduced, stored in a retrieval system, or transmitted, in any form, or by any means, electronic, mechanical, photocopying, recording or otherwise, without the prior permission of the publishers.

Copyright © 2024 Susan A. Ngong

ISBN: 9781763591868

This book is sold subject to the conditions that it shall not, by way of trade or otherwise, be lent, re-sold, hired out or otherwise circulated without the publisher's prior consent in any form of binding or cover other than in which it is published and without a similar condition including the condition being imposed on the subsequent purchaser.

Cover design, typesetting and layout: Africa World Books
Unit 3, 57 Frobisher St, Osborne Park, WA 6017
P.O. Box 1106 Osborne Park, WA 6916

Edited by Susan G Scott AE

DEDICATION

To God Almighty the great mentor who is always there when am in need. Thank you for guiding me and giving me strength in my everyday life and spiritual journey. Thank you for always looking out for me and being therefor for me. Thank you for making all this happen and end up with a good outcome. I love you Lord. God.

In memory of my dear parents; Dr. Bellario Ahoy Ngong and Rose Ayak Deng, both were great inspiration to my life journey. Thank you for being there for me and surely will never forget your tender loving nature.

To my children, there is more to the world than it appears. Always push yourself to do better and be better. Endeavor to rely on God Almighty for your inspiration.

ABOUT THE AUTHOR

Advocate/Lawyer and Lecturer,
University of Juba, School of Law

During my undergrad I had the opportunity to intern with different government institutions such as South Sudan's Human Rights Commission, The Constitution Review Commission and got to practise in a renowned law firm. I graduated with a law degree in 2014 from Uganda Christian University and started working at Liberty Advocates where I got my advocate licence a year later. In 2021, I graduated from University of Juba with a master's degree from the University of Juba.

I enjoy writing and was best in essay writing in primary school. Some of the literature I came across were Chinua Achebe's *Things fall apart*, The Merchant of Venice, and the Harry Potter series by J.K.Rowling. I appreciate the artwork and excellent masterpieces these incredible writers have produced. They have inspired me greatly and shaped my desire for literature.

The reason why I chose to venture into this genre is

more of passion for the arts. Imagination can create beautiful forms of art that can be entertaining as well as expressive with a message in the end or just an adventure. I hope the "*Adventures of Akana; the Ancestral Bequest*" is a gift for those who enjoy exploring imaginative realms and adventure.

There is reference to scientific phenomena such as the Pangea which was a massive supercontinent that formed between 320 million and 195 million years ago. At that time, the earth did not have seven continents but instead was surrounded by a single ocean called Panthalassa. This is to toy with the idea that there is so much connection between the present and the past. What if we could get a chance to move from the present to the past just to see with our own eyes the beauty of nature?

CONTENTS

Acknowledgement — 9
Preface — 11
Introduction — 15

Chapter One: Akana From Kush — 17

Chapter Two: Endangered Species: Alpha 4.0 — 31

Chapter Three: The Swap — 45

Chapter Four: Menelek *(Nife-En-Ank)* And The Hidden Kingdom — 59

ACKNOWLEDGEMENT

In order for such a beautiful work of literature to come into existence there is always a support system. Either emotionally, literally or in some way, each step is valuable and each input precious. I would like to appreciate my husband for his tremendous support and constantly encouraging me to put my talent into writing. The rest of my family; my brothers for believing in my capabilities.

I extend appreciation and recognition to all scholarly works written and stored on ancient African Civilization and African history. I believe if information is recorded written and made available to the public its part of preservation of culture and hence its continuance. This book elects to be part of showing and reminding the world the history of one of the fascinating ancient civilizations which had existed in Northern Africa and other continents. So, we Africans did not start from zero for long before European colonization and slavery, we had immense knowledge in most disciplines including mathematics, physics and medicine. This can be evidenced through the history of the Kemetic culture in ancient Egypt and Ethiopia.

I would also like to express my gratitude to African World Books for editing and publishing this book and Peter Lual Deng for his continuous support in pushing the publication of the book. To Come Let's Read Initiative represented by Ajak Kuol, your contribution and support are very much appreciated. My colleagues and students many thanks for your contributions. And finally, to South Sudan for giving me the inspiration to create such a lovely piece of art.

PREFACE

The Adventures of Akana; The Ancestral Bequest is a figment of my imagination. This is an adventure of a young African female who is discovered to be carrying a dominant gene that determines the anatomy of the next humanoid species known as Alfa 4.0, the endangered species. She came to carry this gene through her great ancestor Menelek, a prince from an ancient realm that dates back as far as three hundred thousand years ago when the first Homo sapiens were discovered in Africa. The Northern parts of Africa, especially Egypt and Ethiopia, are embedded with history of the most ancient civilisation that spread wide across part of the Asian continent that is modern day India. Archaeologists and scholars have made several discoveries of literary works on the ancient civilisation that we treasure as sources of references.

At a young age I always marvelled at science fiction and fantasy films, to the point that I could imagine myself to be a superhero one day. I was a bit dismayed that there were not so many African superheroes who children and the public could emulate or draw inspiration from. Probably our stories or folktales are not told much because there were no records of the very many untold stories that occurred a hundred thousand years ago.

This book is in the fantasy literature genre and may have some aspects of science fiction. The novel is intended to have a series of adventures of a young African woman known as Akana, who hails from the Republic of Kush and was discovered, by an international group known as the Decagon Illusion, to be carrying the Alpha 4.0 gene. Their main mission was to extract the Alpha 4.0 humanoid species (the endangered species) and relocate it to a new headquarters for her safety and further experiments. There has since been some tension in the Decagon group where some members had been compromised by The Circle, an association of billionaires who have the main intention of controlling the world and world events. They prefer the world as is, with them in control of power and resources, so the idea of an Alpha 4.0, who contains the determining DNA of the next humanoid species that would probably change the world's status and outlook, is not their cup of tea. So, this has led The Circle to try to sabotage the Decagon Illusion's mission several times.

Luckily for Akana she survives through the help of very advanced technology and makes it to the new headquarters of the Decagon Illusion in India. It is here that she manages to meet her ancestor who bequeaths her a hidden kingdom, that is a whole new world altogether. The air molecules, flora and fauna of this new world, are so peculiar and so novel that they are second to none in the real world. Akana also inherits the duties and responsibilities of Earth's guardianship and vast knowledge in technology and agriculture. So many adventures and so many series of discoveries that will make a great contribution to modern technology, medicine and sociology await Akana in her journeys to different worlds, realms and time dimensions.

Some of the characters' names, especially from the Republic of Kush, are inspired by the scholarly work written by Faheem Judah-El D.D *Excerpt of Ancient Kemetic Names for children and adults*. All characters are fictitious and any resemblance to real people or places is purely coincidental. In a nutshell, literary works of this genre are intended purely for entertainment purposes and to create some kind of inspiration to those with incredible imaginations. It is suitable for all audiences, especially children who are at a level of improving their literature in essay writing for it to become very rich in vocabulary.

INTRODUCTION

The intention of this fantasy is to elevate the idea of a female of African heritage having the abilities to change the world and contribute greatly to science. She has the capability to inherit and rule a kingdom. Women have, since time immemorial, been considered the weaker gender. Our African cultures especially, are still fighting for women's rights to politics, inheritance and so on. Ideally, I relate to the character Akana as a very strong Alpha female of African descent capable of saving the world. Akana is considered a superhero.

Chapter 1: 'Akana from Kush' introduces the audience to the main character Akana from the Republic of Kush. Akana is from a normal twentieth century family with the father being the bread winner and her mother a housewife. Akana gets an education up to the level of a degree, but unfortunately she loses both her parents. She is now all alone, in a regular job with a low income. She even tries content creation in social media in the hopes of earning side income but fails. She also attends a science symposium.

Chapter2: Alpha 4.0 (the endangered species) The

science symposium results in something positive for Akana. This is where the panelists realise the magnificent mind of Akana because those are the factors they were looking for in identifying their Alpha 4.0. Also, they had the aid of a very special compass that is evidence of a highly sophisticated early civilisation technology as will be discovered in the final chapter. The other members were quickly alerted to their discovery, including the president of the Republic of Kush who had signed a treaty to that effect.

Chapter 3: The swap; This chapter introduces another high-tech device where Patel, one of the scientists from the symposium, employs the use of a cloning device that is so fast and efficient. Akana is in awe of the result; her clone is identical. The president and Patel tactfully plan to successfully swap the real Akana with her clone. This shows a very concerned, dedicated president who wants to ensure the safety of one of her citizens.

Chapter 4: Menelek and the Ancestral Bequest. This is the final chapter where the gist of the novel comes to light. Akana finally meets her ancestor Menelek who was a prince in the ancient civilisation. She inherits a whole new world and treasure, making her the first trillionaire the world has ever heard of

CHAPTER ONE

Akana from Kush

The mind is a very interesting entity on its own that can be used as a tool to solve many of life's problems. When we are in stressful situations, we involve our minds in brainstorming activities that would possibly make the problem go away or make the situation better. The world is in constant change and improvement where there are a lot of discoveries scientifically and technologically. For instance, where would we be if someone hadn't invented the telephone, computer, vehicles, medicines for cure of a variety of diseases and so on? The common thing about these discoveries is the presence of a human being, a human brain and a God-given mind; a conscience that thinks and creates. So, the real question here is what kind of mind do you have? A jammed one, a dead one or one that is constantly creating and solving a lot of problems? Let us take a tour into Miroe, the capital city of the Republic of Kush.

This is a story about a content creator who went through a lot of difficulties before she fully breached the whole deal of creation. Akana was born into a typical twentieth century African family, with the father the bread winner and mother a housewife. She went through the standard primary, secondary and university level of education and found a regular job as is required in society.

Growing up in the social media world, everyday life is governed by your smart phone. You wake up in the middle of the night and you are surely tempted to go through your social media feeds just browsing to keep your mind busy and so it goes on during the day when you are bored or just chilling. There are usually short comedic skits that leave you laughing in the end or music videos of dancing or mimicking voices just for fun. The peculiar thing about Akana is she never started as a content creator; she never even dreamed of such a career path or livelihood.

Akana's major at the university was law, and she became a licensed lawyer working at a renowned law firm with low wages, barely surviving the ever-rising economy and inflation. She also tried applying to various other institutions such as NGOs, oil companies, regular companies and banks but with no success. It turns out that securing such jobs requires connections like an uncle or a friend or a father but with no such links you are most likely going to end up in an economic crunch. As society has trained her and tuned her brain, you get a good college education and apply for a good paying job; that's it, there could be no other way out. Or so she thought. Her father was her main goal pusher; he was the one that set her off on her legal career path, always boasting of how it is an esteemed profession and well paying too, actually one of the four most respected careers in the country. You were either a politician, a doctor, a lawyer or engineer. Anything else is entrepreneurship, without any explainable source of wealth. You can be an internationally successful model and become famous and that's the only way you would have a national reception at the airport.

Her social life was no different to her career. After a few years of dating and going out with different guys there had not been any stable relationship because she realised that most men had basic ways of thinking. Akana's mind was at a different level and she usually surprised herself with the dreams she had and the places her subconscious took her when she was in a deep sleep.

Beautiful minds are rare but there exists in a lifetime numerous genius minds: those that put their thoughts into actions and those that have never tried, or left their dreams as dreams. All in all, Akana was still finding her way around love. It was around those years of self-development that misfortune struck her pathway. She lost both her parents at different times through mysterious ailments. Akana went into a cocoon of sadness for a few years where her brain was jammed with questions, and she found it hard to move on in the crazy economy without any support.

They say necessity is the mother of all inventions. So, it was through this sad phase and rough and tough times that Akana needed to get out of her situation, but how? They also say when you are swallowing a bitter pill and you have no choice but to go through it, then think of a happy place, imagine it, fashion it in your brain and live it. This, of course, can only work if you literally remove yourself from reality and live in this imaginary ideal place. Because this is the real world, it's impossible to move spiritually and physically into a world that exists entirely in your mind's realm. So, she started with something more achievable. She used her phone to create videos and post them through social media. She was not sure whether it could make her money so fast but it was a trial. Her main aim at this point was to get recognition through the videos. She continued working in a regular job during the day for survival, as she explored this digital world with no positive results for several months.

If you were asked simply to describe your happy place, a place where your mind goes to briefly get away from reality, what would it be? I guess most people would like a place where they have absolute control or authority, a place where there is plenty of money, food or gold. A serene and peaceful environment. A place where you have already achieved what you lack and desire to have. According to

Akana it was a state where she was already successful and had attained all that she desired. As she was exploring the social media world, her main goal was to create something unique and quite different but that was not easy. Everything she tried had already been created somewhere else and it was exhausting finding content and posting it almost every day without any economic improvement. She slept hungry for two days, using her feeding allowances to buy some equipment in support of a video she was creating. This went on and on and it felt like a bubble. She felt like a slave in this digital world. One of those days when she was exploring the internet, she came across an advertisement for a scientific symposium looking for young brilliant minds who would like to attend. Well, it looked authentic and was just the following week. So she decided to go.

In case it was going to be a trap or a boring lecture, she brought a friend along. The symposium was located at one of the best hotels in her town, Miroe, at the riverside. The venue was breathtaking, with marbled floors and huge well-designed chandeliers hanging from the ceiling. The reception area was well furnished with modern decor, comfortable waiting sofas you could almost sink inside. A well-dressed lady approached Akana and asked if she was here for the science conference and she was ushered into the conference room. Well, it was a normal conference room with seats organised in three sections with a long table on the stage where the panel of presenters was going to sit.

There were no posters on the wall, just a single billboard-like poster placed above the presenters. The words *The Evolution of the Human brain; the future of science* sat above an image of the human brain. The panelists were three white men whom Akana came to know later in the day to be Europeans and an African native, a local from Akana's area, who worked for the government of the Republic of Kush.

As the morning progressed, the conference room filled, although there were still empty seats at the back. A young Asian gentleman was distributing the agenda to everyone who was seated. The presentation started once the hall was three-quarters filled. The African host introduced himself and welcomed the visitors. The presentation was all science, which Akana found difficult, but it was made more understandable by the pictures projected on a screen.

Well, what intrigued her and other participants most was the examples of discovery of genius minds by famous scientists throughout history.

During the tea break, Akana and her friend Samira joked about how everything has been invented and no room for new inventions. Samira was Akana's on-and-off hanging-out buddy. They were not best friends per se but had met at a friend's birthday party and found a common meeting of the minds. Samira worked at an NGO well paid job and could afford travelling occasionally, but funnily enough, she had never tried to get Akana a job at her organisation despite Akana's constant request. In life there are those kinds of people who love hanging with you but would not like to see you doing better than them. They would rather be ahead. Akana came to realise that this was part of life. As the two girls were conversing heartily, the young bespectacled Asian gentleman approached them and smiled, introducing himself as a scholar from India with a major in neuroscience.

He did not say much but was hoping that they could stay for a short quiz after the symposium. It would take only half an hour of their time, and Akana and Samira both agreed since they did not have tight schedules for the day. The rest of the presentations went smoothly, and after a brief lunch some attendees left and those who had volunteered to take the quiz were taken into another room.

Akana and her friend entered the smaller room with tables arranged as if in an exam room. Each person sat at their own table. There was a piece of paper on top of the table with a pencil, eraser and sharpener just adjacent to the paper. As Akana sat at her table, she scanned the room and briefly counted the participants, about twenty, around the same age as she was. She looked down at the sheet of paper and saw only three questions, each with ample space for jotting down the answer. Samira decided to sit in front of Akana, probably hoping that she would not copy her answers and hoping they could be a kind of a reward after the symposium. She always thought of Akana as disadvantaged, and she was convinced that she was as dumb as a dodo. Little did she know that if your success comes earlier than others, it does not mean the others are stupid and incapable of succeeding. This is thanks to the uniqueness of each individual and phenomenon in the universe and time. Each individual on Earth is allocated their own time span, based on their environment and other factors.

The presenters welcomed the participants to the short quiz and thanked them for their time to participate. They gave very simple instructions that there were three questions to be answered in accordance with the participant's views. When finished they should raise their hand and the examiners would pick up the answer sheets. They were also required to indicate their name and email address for future contact. There was no mention of any rewards or any kind of recruitment of the 'winners". All they said was that it was for a questionnaire to help conclude the findings to the presentation they had made that day. *Oh well,* thought Akana, *it would not hurt to help these nice white men conclude their research or whatever they were looking for.*

The first question seemed easy but very weird. It said, 'What would you do if you thought you were being chased by a grizzly bear in the forest; What is your survival instinct?'

The second question, according to Akana, was somewhat complicated and she instantly regretted not paying attention during the presentation. It read, 'Which side of your brain do you usually engage in solving problems; the right brain or the left brain?'

And the third question could not have been stranger, 'What colour was lingering in your mind this morning before coming to this Science symposium?' Whatever the presenters were looking for could not be clearer but it could also be plausible to conclude that they were looking for diversity in the individual perception.

Akana could not know that whatever answers she provided might lead to a series of events that would change her life for the best. This was it; this was the opportunity that the universe presented to someone stuck in a rut, in an economic crunch or someone who was lonely and had no one to advise and console her. Her adventures would in turn lead to new discoveries that would change the world's paradigm and create new inventions and hence opportunities.

As she read the first question a second time, so many scenarios started building up in her mind, as she came to realise that the question was asking what would do if you thought you were being chased by a grizzly bear. The best answer was to simply stop thinking, then the grizzly bear would automatically disappear. But according to Akana there was more to this question than that simple implication; if it was possible to create a scenario in your mind of a very scary creature such as the grizzly bear pursuing you and wanting to kill you, then you could also create in the same mind a scenario where you suddenly stopped running and turned yourself into a scarier creature than the grizzly bear, maybe twice or thrice bigger with horns and a terrifying groan. That would have automatically startled the poor bear to run for its life. Give the bear a few blows and wound him with your huge claws and finally end it life by tearing its head off using your massive teeth. As vivid as her imagination was, she quickly jotted down what her mind was giving her.

The second question was brain racking, but Akana chose to answer in the most basic way. Usually, when she was faced with a problem, she employed her brain and probably her whole being in looking for ways to solve it. Could it have been the right brain or the left brain? She could never know, but what she knew was that she could sometimes involve the supernatural entities in case of severity of the issue. So she answered that she involved both the right and the left and any other part of the brain that is not physically located inside the skull.

The answer to the third question, according to Akana, was the colour of a lit up electric bulb. White, yellow or orange, depending on the type of the bulb used. Ever since she was younger, when the word 'science' was mentioned, that was the colour that always appeared in her mind. So that was the answer she wrote.

When she had finished, she looked around the room and

some participants were still jotting away while others were holding their jaws, critically thinking. When she looked up at her friend Samira she saw her using her mobile phone trying to google the correct answers; the examiners saw that but they seemed not to mind at all. Akana raised her hand and her paper was taken from her. She was not confident or cautious of her answers because she knew that there was no competition or any rewards coming after words. This was just a summary survey.

After Akana had handed in her quiz, she went to the bathroom to wait for Samira. While she was in one of the female stalls she could hear a male voice coming from the male bathrooms, just next to the ladies' room. The accent was deep Indian, seemingly communicating on a cell phone.

"Am sure, Master. I cross checked the coordinates; the latitude and longitude are leading us to this particular town." There was a little pause for response from other side. The voice said, "The symposium went well and in fact the quiz is going on right now. As in accordance with my dream, the chosen one is of African descent but not quite sure if it is a male or female."

Then suddenly, Akana heard a toilet flush and could not make out anything more of the conversation and after that there was silence. When she was done with the facilities she washed up and left. She immediately met Samira just outside the corridor, trying to text her whereabouts.

The two girls then left the hotel, returning to their residences. Akana could not stop wondering what the symposium and the short quiz was all about, and the strange conversation she had heard while she was in the washroom. Just out of curiosity she tried googling the organisation that had conducted the symposium and lo and behold she could not find anything. No trace of them at all. She tried searching the name of the Indian gentleman and nothing came up, except for a few similar names from social media accounts with no recognisable picture. She wondered why the government would invite strange entities for a science project. What could they be looking for? She hoped not guinea pigs for their science experiments. Akana consoled herself anyway, as she was sure that the answers she had given were not brilliant enough to lure her into any such situation.

A month went by as she continued with her usual boring life, until she stumbled upon an email sent to her three weeks earlier. Akana had gotten into the habit of scrolling through her social media feeds every single day and watching videos with little or no attention at all to her emails. The email was from the science symposium, inviting her for a brunch to socialise with the members of the panel before they left the country. The day the organisers were supposed to leave was not mentioned in the email, but the brunch had been two weeks earlier. So she had missed it. She sat there contemplating what to do and chose to reply to the email that she had been attending a funeral of a relative, which was why she could not make it for the brunch. She did not think that her email would be replied to, because they would be long gone by then. It was around nine on a Saturday morning; after replying to the email she decided to take a quick shower and dress up to start her day. When she came out of the shower she scrolled through her phone and found out that her email had been replied ten minutes ago. It read that the organisers of the symposium were still around and would not mind catching up that afternoon in the same hotel where the symposium had been held. With no hesitation she quickly dressed up and went to the hotel. She realised that her life was not going to change, just sitting down and pouting on how unfair it really was.

CHAPTER TWO

Endangered Species: Alpha 4.0

This encounter marks the next chapter of Akana's life where it took a different turn—change from normal sluggish life and stagnancy. The adventures she would experience would forever change her life for the better. The knowledge of so many hidden issues of the world would be overwhelming. She would meet peculiar people that were thought to be from fiction or children's fairytales. In the first chapter we realised that there have been so many discoveries in technology, medicine and general lifestyle to the point that there could not possibly be any further new discoveries in this day and age. We were all wrong! There exists in our world realms that have never been uncovered before, only due to lack of proper knowledge and tools to access them. There is always a key that is required to open a closed door. Akana would come to know her true purpose and destiny.

The organisers of the symposium could not leave Africa just yet, especially this town that they had been led to, because they felt they were still missing their piece to the puzzle. The reason why the credentials of some of the panelists did not exist on the internet (as Akana would know later) was not because they were not actual scientists, but because their mission was classified. Some governments of various countries, especially high-level officials, did know about these people and their missions and had signed treaties of non-disclosure of their existence or their mission. Some of the billionaires of the world were part of this because this was how they got the resources to finance their operation.

Akana appeared at the hotel as agreed. She was told to wait in the lobby and after about ten minutes, the bespectacled young Indian scholar approached her. She could almost recognise his voice as the one that was coming from the washrooms during the quiz. Before she could think any more, she was ushered into the garden lounge. A white woman smiled and introduced herself as Grace, extending her hand to Akana to greet her. The Indian she came to know as Patel Kumar.

"Miss Akana…we would like to thank you for taking the time to attend our symposium. How was the presentation?" Grace said almost immediately, leaving no room for awkward silence.

"The presentation was very good…the most exciting part was the short quiz; it was weird but fun."

Patel flipped the pages of his notebook as he looked

at Akana and muttered, "Dominance". Akana looked at him, confused. He continued, "Your answer to your first question: what would you do if you thought your being chased by a grizzly bear? What is your survival instinct? …' dominance…after describing your encounter with a grizzly bear and since it's an imagination you will stop and turn yourself into a more scary creature with horns and massive teeth, tear his head off and it immediately ceases to exist. So your survival instinct is dominance. You would rather face the danger, tackle it and dominate the situation."

Grace looked on, in awe at the answers that Akana had given. After Patel read out her answer to the second question she added, "The human brain is divided into two halves: the right brain and the left one. There's a myth that suggests some people are left-brained, while others are right-brained. However, despite their contrasting styles, the two halves of your brain are connected by brain fibres and work together."

Akana felt a sigh of relief that, based on the answers she had given they were not stupid at all. Coming from a legal background as opposed to scientific one, the only knowledge of human anatomy she had ever acquired was at high school level. Furthermore, she thought to herself, both disciplines do require the use of a brain in calculating, reasoning and even imagination. Her train of thought was cut short when Patel asked her to elaborate on what she meant by the colour of science being the color of a lit-up bulb.

Akana froze a bit as she swallowed her spit and sheepishly blurted, " To be real honest with you I came up with that light bulb analogy to impress you guys in order to look like a genius because usually ideas are represented by lit up light bulbs; and also in case there would be some kind of a reward offered to the participants," she smiled and went on. "I have a degree in law and any knowledge of science I have ever acquired was at a high school level. I have never worked in a lab dicing things up or mixing chemicals, neither do I know the composition of various chemicals and their reaction. I was just accompanying a friend." She peered nervously at her audience who were keenly listening to her.

Patel smiled and laughed lightly, amazed at her brutal honesty and purity. They each ordered tea and were sipping as they conversed. It was during their interesting discussions that the topic of aliens and celestial bodies came up.

"I think aliens are not a myth at all. The story is not told right in films. You see, movies depict aliens as very intelligent beings with elongated skulls and huge dark eyes with grey skin, invading Earth and taking over the human race one day. According to me there is no other form of intelligent life that has been registered in any other planets so far; so, I believe these 'aliens' are actual human beings that have evolved over two thousand or more years from today and they would come to earth in disc-like ships because those ships are probably time travelling machines. The future human race that is the 'aliens' would travel back through time and appear before us, the Homo sapiens, and invade our time space for whatever reasons. Into the very far future I believe we would have invented time travelling machines," Akana said enthusiastically.

Grace and Patel were speechless since they had never heard of such a theory before, and were amazed by her vivid imagination. The Indian gentleman excused himself to the bathroom while Grace could not stop staring at Akana while listening keenly to her opinions.

"Mmmmh. So, Miss Akana, the version of the evolved human race, according to you, would look like the aliens we see in the movies?"

"Probably, or any other version, but there could be no smoke without fire. Our ancestors were thought to be apes, right?" Akana replied.

Grace could not follow any more and almost immediately her mind went to the mission they had come to do. This young African lady was giving fresh ideas more than any other participants they had encountered, and had the most vivid and unique imagination. She could be the one they were looking for.

The classified mission was to appear and conduct a symposium within the coordinates they had been given, to find the one with the most unique personality and imagination. You can see how at any level of human evolution, from the Homo habilis to Homo erectus to the Homo sapiens, there was that one individual that carried the evolutionary gene (DNA) that started the chain of novel species. In other words, she was the father (or in this case the mother) of the next upgraded human species. She carried that gene that would replicate, duplicate and mutate its cells to a novel species. This would be the first time that such discoveries were ever made and that was why the mission was classified. There was a group that we will later know as the Decagon Illusion, all after one objective of saving the universe and their experiments and discoveries led them to a possible existence of the "alpha four point zero" a gene that would determine the next level of human species.

Akana was not prepared for the next turn of events. As she was sipping her tea at the hotel and enjoying the afternoon, she kept wondering why Grace and Patel had left the table all of a sudden and had taken a while away. She thought that maybe she bored them with ridiculous assertions and opinions. Maybe she should tone it down a bit on the ramblings. She could not control her mind but she could surely control her mouth. If only she knew what was going on in the background.

Patel came back to the table, suggesting that Akana should order lunch. He pulled out a white cloth and wiped her forehead as he had noticed that she was sweating from the hot weather in the Garden Lounge. It was a hot afternoon and they had moved into the cooler dining room. Then Patel disappeared for a second time, while Akana helped herself from the lunch buffet. After choosing what she would like to eat on her plate she sat in the restaurant eating alone, uneasy and wondering where the duo was and what they could be up to. Before she could finish her meal, Patel and Grace walked in with their plates of food, joining Akana at her table. After they were done with their meal, they asked Akana to join them in another private room.

As they were marching through the corridor, Akana grabbed Patel's arm and whispered, "Is everything alright? Am I in some kind of trouble?"

Patel simply assured her that everything was alright. When they walked into the room there were other members of the panel that Akana recalled from the symposium and the man from the government who had launched it. There was an open laptop on the table in the middle of the room and a projector connected to it. Akana was told to take one of the seats right in front of the laptop so she could face the projection on the wall. Her heart was pounding slightly and anxiety filled her whole body. Before her mind could wander further, a tall thin gentleman with blond shabby hair approached Akana and greeted her with respect. His attire was casual, a greyish suit with black shiny shoes.

He then proceeded with the presentation, "I would like to first introduce myself. My name is Dr. Henry Maiser, an expert in neurology. Just to keep you out of suspense, when we came to conduct the symposium, we were actually on a confidential mission, in simpler terms, secret operation.

There is an organisation known as the Decagon Illusion which consists of prominent members of the society that have been overseeing various world issues and occurrences. We have scientists who have been conducting experiments over the years and especially in the human anatomy and evolution theories. Our findings have led us to believe that every point of evolutionary level, there is a dominant gene that exists on an individual that starts the evolutionary chain; that is the Alpha 4.0. There are also theorists who believe that the DNA and ideas, opinions of the Alpha 4.0 could be a key to various unexplainable phenomena and unexplored worlds."

Dr. Henry stopped clicking on the slides of his presentation and briefly looked at a very confused Akana who had no idea what was going on.

"Let me be as precise as possible. You see, Ms. Akana, the quiz you took part in three weeks ago during the symposium was tailored to track down the Alpha 4.0. Based on your answers, the results were more than we expected. We were told that the Alpha 4.0 would give very intelligent, imaginative, out-of-this-world responses. And we do possess a very rare compass that gave us the coordinates of the town where the Alpha 4.0 could be found: Meroe town in the Republic of Kush in Africa. It even gave us the exact street and the hotel to book. The only thing the compass could not tell was the gender. Some of us, especially I, thought we could be looking for a male. Anyway, we do have our DNA detectors we brought with us and we used a small sample of your DNA to detect that dominant gene and it was a match. Our device is very fast and it can take just thirty minutes for the results to come out. In case you were wondering how we obtained the sample of your DNA, it was through your sweat. We sent Patel here to pretend to wipe the sweat from your forehead using a handkerchief." Dr. Henry paused to usher in the next presenter.

A lean older woman with greyish white hair came to the front and introduced herself as Dr. Hilde Wagner. Akana noticed tiny freckles on her high cheek bones as she introduced herself.

"I am not really a scientist, by the way, but an advocate for the preservation of endangered species. Rare genes such as those that Alpha 4.0 possesses are considered unique and most likely endangered. There is the possibility of danger such as very powerful enemies that could destroy future generations, or a science corporation that would take advantage of you, using you as a guinea pig and torturing your life forever. This is why we chose to be as discrete as possible and make the mission classified."

Suddenly there were sirens a short distance away, approaching the hotel. Akana's heart skipped a beat and she thought probably there was going to be some kind of trouble.

The other members in the room started fidgeting and moving chairs and rearranging the room, placing one of the big chairs in the middle and two smaller chairs at either side. The three chairs faced the chairs of Akana and the other panelists, seated with a distance of two feet between them. It then dawned on Akana that there was someone important about to join them. The door to the room swung open and three men dressed in black suits, wearing dark sunglasses, walked in ushering everyone to stand. Everyone obeyed meekly and in walked a very excited Her Excellency the President of the Republic of Kush, Madam Kandakes Menetnashte. Akana was shocked as she had never met the president this close, just two feet away. There was a younger well-dressed lady who followed, carrying the president's purse, notebook and phone. There was total silence as the president took her seat in one of the big chairs set across the room, and her assistant followed. The bodyguards, dressed in black, positioned themselves at either side of the room while the other stood at the rear end of the room with the backs of Akana's facing them. After that, everyone else was directed to sit.

"All protocol observed. I would like to first welcome the Decagon Illusion group to Kush; feel free, this is your home. I am glad that the pursuit of the long-awaited endangered species Alpha 4.0 has come to an end. And for it to be found under Kushite soil. So, as we abide by the international treaty signed between Kush and Decagon Illusion, we give permission to hand over the Alpha 4.0 for its protection, as it is considered an endangered species and on the other hand ready to receive our consideration."

She smiled and a gentleman from the Decagon Illusion group handed a brief case to the private secretary of the president before mentioning that another additional three billion dollars had already been wired to the government account. The private secretary opened the brief case and from Akana's end she could see a hundred dollars in bundles, probably a million. All her life Akana had never thought she could be this expensive! She could not even afford payment of rent of her apartment on time. It would be rude to interrupt the president, so she waited for her time.

"Young lady, what is your name?" She peered at Akana from her spectacles. She was in her early fifties and had not aged a bit. She was tall, dark-skinned with a little pot belly. She liked wearing very bright official attire, consisting of dresses, trouser suits or skirt suits with a matching hat or shoes occasionally.

"Your excellency, my name is Akana Khenti," she muttered.

"Akana, I would like to be very clear to you that you are doing a great service to your country. There is a possibility your genes and contributions to the development of science shall be exceptional and we Kushites will always consider you as a hero. We will make sure you are taken care of during the operations of the mission and in anything government will be liable."

Such assurances made Akana a little calm and collected

but there was still that looming fear of the unknown. Did she have the right to refuse to participate? she thought to herself. That was not going to happen at any time as she was amazed by the title they had given her: Endangered Species Alpha 4.0. She was now under the protection of the state and international organisations, and any withdrawals at this stage would only expose her to unnecessary danger. By this time all the members of Decagon Illusion had already been informed, even those as far away as Rome.

Then the president gently asked Akana in her native language if she had any problems, and asked her about her parents and family. Akana informed her that both her parents had died and she was an only child living in a one-bedroomed apartment. Her relatives lived far away and only contacted her once in a while. The president took the contact details of close relatives from her to inform them later of the whereabouts of Akana, leaving out the details of the secret missions. She informed the uncle that Akana would be working with the government from today and would be sent on an international mission. Akana informed the president that she had nothing with her and her bank account was registering zero dollars, in case she would be required to travel. Her Excellency laughed lightly at Akana's request and told her that everything would be taken care of, and to follow her into the lobby before she left.

She then broke the tension in the room saying in English, "Alpha 4.0 is now under the legal custody of the

Decagon Illusion. The Republic of Kush gives their authority for her transfer to the headquarters in Europe."

They all agreed and retired to their rooms, blissfully unaware of any suspicious activities.

The Decagon Illusion is an alliance of most national governments, some individual billionaires and prominent religious figures. They have often been misrepresented as members of occult groups, but they are something more than that. The purpose of forming the group was to monitor, supervise and guard the human race in case of any imminent world calamities. They are indeed a secret group whose intentions are purely noble.

But as the world progressed, other groups came up such as the ritualistic Circle who aggressively want to control the world and world events. If there was a species of human race that could presumably change the world it would be such a blow to their "kingdom". They have thrived in these centuries because of their capability of being at the top of everything. They control any upcoming world events at various fields and needless to say are very wealthy. In the past three decades the Decagon Illusion have come to realise that there are members in their group that have been infiltrated by The Circle and have been giving out classified information and now they have become aware of a search for Alpha 4.0 whom they refer to as the "chosen one".

CHAPTER THREE

The Swap

After the briefing, the president stood up to leave while everyone immediately stood to show their respect. Akana followed the president as she had requested and they went into another room. which appeared to be a private VIP room with a washroom inside. The private secretary disappeared into the washrooms while the president and her bodyguards and Akana remained in the room. Patel came in and with a sharp pair of scissors snipped off a small portion of Akana's hair. Akana often liked leaving her hair natural and kempt or wore cornrows if she pleased at times.

The Indian gentleman took the hair sample of the supposed "Endangered Species" and hurriedly entered the other gentlemen's washroom. By this time the private secretary came out wearing a totally different outfit, more like the uniform worn by the waitresses in that hotel. She quickly handed over her clothes to Akana, who was directed by the president to quickly change. Akana obeyed, though she had so many questions running through her mind.

When she tried on the private secretary's clothes, they were a perfect fit, then she looked into the mirror at the same Kushitic-dark complexion and they were very alike. The only slight difference was Akana was a bit lighter; the difference between them was very subtle. She came out of the room and was given a wig to wear, which was apparently hers, too. Akana was instructed to give her clothes to Patel, who was in the other washroom.

Ten minutes later Patel walked out of the room holding a lady's hand. The lady was a pure and perfect clone of Akana. She wore Akana's clothes and it was as if she was looking in the mirror. The real Akana got up and approached her clone and she could not believe it; they were truly identical. Then Patel instructed Akana to speak; to state one full sentence. She introduced herself and her clone, in a split second, mimicked her voice and started speaking like her.

"This is very sophisticated and advanced technology not yet released to the world. The invention is still in the experimental stages. With a small sample of the DNA—", Patel cut himself short, assuring Akana that he would explain more another time because they needed to move fast out of the room. Time was of the essence.

The president then held the real Akana by the hand and told her to follow her instructions carefully. "The Decagon

Illusion has been compromised by The Circle, who are already aware of the mission to retrieve Alpha 4.0 from Kush. They have been following closely and they do have spies. So, for your safety you will leave the room as my private secretary. Your clone will leave with Patel to handover as Alpha 4.0 to the Decagon Illusion group. So, we need to move on as fast as possible. We will explain more when you are in a safe place."

A total of twenty minutes was spent in this VIP room, then the president left the room with her "private secretary" and her bodyguards. As they reached the reception area, members of the Decagon were across the lobby waving at her as she left in her vehicle. The Decagon had no idea that there was an exchange because the clone of Akana looked identical. Patel then approached the other members of the Decagon informing them that it was already approaching seven o'clock and Akana needed to take a rest before the next day's travel to Europe.

So far, through the years, there had been five attempts to retrieve the Alpha 4.0 and every time they came too close, something happened. There was either an aeroplane crash, disappearance of the aeroplane, hurricane or an epidemic of some sort. Decagon Illusion had undertaken their own research and discovered that two members of the alliance had been influenced by The Circle, including their headquarters located in Europe.

A new location for the group was established without

the knowledge of the alleged whistle blowers. The other members vowed to continue to work with them, but kept them in the dark with some information. This time round, they would get ahead to make sure that Alpha.4.0 would not be harmed at all.

Akana reached the presidential palace at around eight in the evening. She was given a room and had the pleasure of dining with the president. This was something really special for Akana. She used to dream of being a hero or a celebrity, meeting prominent people, and now she was right here, having a meal with the president and going on a top-secret mission. She always thought she would die poor, or at least average, because the only way to survive in this day and age was through connections and as her parents were both deceased, she saw no way out. Who knew, after tears and loss of hope, that the universe would just swoop in and select you from a crowd like a needle in a haystack and lift you up? All this she owed to God. He surely had a role in this.

The president announced a detour to Akana's journey. She would not be going to Europe, but to a new location which would be revealed only after she arrived. She was to travel this same night at midnight via a private presidential jet. She was ushered into her room where she was to take a shower and rest a little bit. She was given a new lady's purse and new fancy clothing. Inside the purse was around thirty thousand dollars, a new expensive phone and Bluetooth earphones.

At around eleven-thirty, Akana entered the vehicle and was escorted to the airport by the president and two of her bodyguards. It took them thirty minutes to reach the airstrip where the private jet was waiting. . She boarded the plane and was surprised to see Patel there handing her a glass of champagne. The president bade her farewell and promised to call her on the phone she had been given.

Akana had so many questions for her Indian companion, especially about what had happened to her clone.

He laughed lightly at her and said, "My dear, you have a lot to learn. Your clone will be travelling in the morning at nine through one of the local airlines with the Decagon group, and I'll be there, but in clone form. I have already instructed my clone on what to do. There would be absolutely nothing to be suspicious about." He peered at Akana who was amazed and keenly sipped her drink. "Anyway, you must be tired and we have a long journey ahead of us." He altered her seat to a position where she should get a good night's sleep.

As she slumbered, a terrible nightmare crept in. She found herself in a small zinc-lined room with three gentlemen and a very pregnant woman, digging inside a sack full of old gold coins, ornaments, gold necklaces, rings, basically treasure one could find inside a treasure chest. They were so shiny that they could not resist stuffing them in their pockets. Then Akana found gold earrings studded with pearls. She raised them to admire them, then almost immediately the room became dark. As they fumbled in the dark, they saw a familiar figure, a pyramid like those constructed by ancient Egyptians, directly above them rotating clockwise while they seemed to be deep down in the looming darkness. There was an eerie harrowing sound of something moving and approaching them. Almost immediately, one of the gentlemen let out a terrifying shriek before the group noticed that his head had been severed and was tumbling on the ground. Then a figure wearing a green gown with a golden mask appeared holding two bloody knives crossed in front of his chest, and started chopping the group mercilessly.

When Akana saw this, she started running out of the room, with others following her, and the eerie figure in pursuit. Outside was a vast field and small houses adjacent to the room. She hid behind the other rooms, with the pregnant woman. They covered their mouths so they could not make any sounds, while loud shrieks could be heard in the distance from the slain gentlemen. They could hear the figure approaching, although its feet were not touching the ground but hovering in the air. As they crouched behind the house, the figure seemed to be scouting around looking for its next victim. Then there was a loud hoot from a train passing nearby. As it turned out in that vast field, there were railway tracks. The eerie figure then fled in fright, probably not wanting to be seen. This was the opportunity Akana and the pregnant woman needed, and they ran tirelessly across the field towards the train. When they reached the railway trucks the train had long gone but there were houses at the other side of the railway lines. A gentleman came out of one of the houses yelling at them to hurry up. Once they reached him, they were advised to throw away all the coins or anything they had found in that room and they did so obediently.

Akana jolted from the nightmare sweating profusely. It took her a split second to realise that she was in a plane as she looked around.

"Oh, you are awake already," said Mr. Patel. "Just in time for landing. Sit in an upright position and tighten your seatbelt." The small aircraft commenced descending and finally landed. When Akana got off the plane, Patel announced emphatically, "Welcome to India."

The chilly morning air brushed against her cheeks. They had landed on an air strip which apparently was not the main airport because a fleet of black SUVs with tinted mirrors was waiting for them in the near distance. A chubby man in a black suit and trench coat approached. He had such a grin that one could notice a gold tooth amidst teeth tainted from too much tobacco smoking.

"Welcome, my compatriots. I hope you had a very comfortable flight?" He extended his hand to both of them, introducing himself to Akana as Rajesh Kumar. He instructed them to enter one of the vehicles. Akana got into one vehicle with Mr. Patel while Rajesh had his own.

As she sat with Patel in the passenger seat Akana could not help but whisper in his ear, "I hope I will not be diced up like a science project in a lab." Patel let out a light chuckle and assured her that there would be nothing like that, and this mission had clauses that prevented such inhumane acts. A few samples of her blood and hair were all that would be required for DNA analysis.

The road they took led up to the mountains, which Akana later knew to be the Northwest of India. The population was thinning as they approached the mountain side, and they reached what she thought was a dead end at the foot of the mountain. Suddenly, the mountain side in front of them started moving vertically, revealing a cave. It seemed like a secret passage into the mountain, and they drove into the darkness with only the headlights on from the vehicles.

Finally, they reached an open space. It was a clearing with the sun's rays streaming through. Up ahead stood a mansion with castle-like features with a driveway leading to the gate. As they approached the gate, the gatekeeper seemed to have recognised the vehicles and he immediately stood up to open the gate. The vehicles quickly streamed in, making a halt at the door of the mansion. Everyone came out of the vehicles. Akana was greeted by a couple of individuals but she could only remember two men from the government and the chubby gentleman who had received them when they landed. It turned out that Rajesh was one of the lucrative entrepreneurs with a billionaire status. His family had been in the business of textile industries for years. So, this mansion was where they carried out their secret operations and managed to house peculiar artefacts, items and instruments that dated back as far as the ancient civilisation. There were several rooms: a showroom which we could say was a museum containing queer things that had never been seen or heard of in real life.

Akana was taken to the dining hall which was organised in such a way that it looked like a restaurant. Kitchen staff were waiting to usher them in for breakfast. It was a buffet, of course, where you could serve yourself whatever you desired. There was the scent of Indian spices in the room, as the lids were removed from the dishes. Akana chose whatever food could be friendly to her stomach without adventuring into spicy foods. She liked the meat-filled samosas with a pinch of chilli, though. After a hearty breakfast she was escorted to her room by Mr. Patel and told to take a shower, rest, and he would come for her in the evening to meet Rajesh at dinner for a short briefing of the mission.

Akana took in a deep breath and said to herself, *This is it, this is where my life drastically turns around.* Who knew that destiny could drop on your doorstep in just a split second, leaving you no room to think? She also had this worrying fear that these were all strangers and anything evil could happen at any moment. Things were happening so fast. Was it all too good to be true? While thoughts were racing through her mind in her room her phone rang. She reached for her purse and retrieved the phone with 'unknown number' across the screen.

She picked up the phone and a very familiar voice warmed her heart. It was her president; she had kept her promise of calling her after all. She wanted to know if she was okay and if she had landed and been received well. Akana responded by confirming that she was okay and had reached the mansion. The president assured her that everything would be alright, that she need not fear since the phone she was given had a GPS tracker inside and could record outside voices and even take videos while the phone was off. She instructed her to carry the phone at all times to any meetings or experiments they were going to do.

"We are watching you, my daughter. Do not feel like you are alone. You are a citizen of Kush. Your safety is our first priority," she finished off by asserting. Akana could not help but let out a sigh of relief. No words had ever seemed as reassuring as those. She carried on confidently, knowing that she was representing her country on a special mission.

Later, Mr. Patel came to collect Akana from her room to go for lunch. He mentioned as a by-the-way that the plane that their clones were on had crashed that morning, less than an hour after takeoff due to technical malfunctions in the plane. Apparently, the airline had just changed their plane to a new one which had a complicated computerised system. There were no survivors. Akana was shocked and devastated at the news but Patel did not seem to be affected at all. They had predicted this move from The Circle Their leader was unknown because they operated secretly. They were a very powerful lethal group rumoured to be harnessing magic from a realm that had not been discovered previously.

As Akana sat down to her meal, she was very melancholic and almost lost her appetite from the terrifying news she had heard. The television right above them in the dining room was showing the breaking news of the plane crash. The wreckage looked so devasting. Patel looked at Akana and saw how she was deeply moved and tried to cheer her up by consoling her that it would have been a close call if they had not thought of cloning her. She still wondered though, if the clone was a real human being and Patel said yes, it was. She was dumbfounded and now knew why the mission was classified. These people were actually dangerous. Rajesh broke the tension by offering to give a tour to Akana of the mysterious items they had managed to obtain over the years.

Akana enjoyed her walk around the mansion and was really awed by the artifacts that do actually exist; the soul gazer that looked like swimming goggles, so that when you wear them you are able to see someone's soul or spirit. The cloning machine which was used by Patel earlier. The special compass that when you whisper the person's or item's name, it shows you the coordinates as quick as lightning. There was the invisible hat that once you wear it, you disappear into thin air and cannot be seen or felt. The belt and amour that were worn by the ancient warriors and kings, acting as shields, which no manner of arrow whatever the design could penetrate. There were several other ancient tools used in agriculture in the olden civilisation that were peculiar but made work easier. There were numerous seashells of various sizes and shapes displayed in translucent jars on the shelves. Other jars contained herbs. As Akana was exploring the jar section, she could not help but wonder at a jar that contained a very tiny human floating in some kind of liquid and Rajesh quickly explained that inasmuch as you heard of giants that walked the earth at one time so, too, there were tiny human-like creatures they actually spewed from another realm when one of the ancient Kings stumbled upon a portal into another world in the heart of the mountains. There were several pots as well as several statues of all shapes and sizes of animals and humans and of humans with animal features. There was a library of old spell books or books that have knowledge over unknown things. So many other things—it was such a large collection, truly a museum. Going through each and every item and its usage would take a week or more. Rajesh then pulled Akana's arm towards a large mirror with a huge diagonal crack running across it.

The mirror had a mysterious frame; thorns crisscrossing all around it forming the entire frame.

"This is the magic mirror. I think you have ever heard of it from your childhood fairytales," said Rajesh jokingly at Akana. "This is also a portal to another world discovered in the old civilisation. There was a very rich merchant who came across it long ago and tried numerous possibilities to make it work but failed and so he sent for foreign astrologers who almost accessed it but their efforts were in vain. They ended up just cracking it." Rajesh pulled out one of the ancient books that he was studying and read out some information about the magic mirror, that it can only be opened by the 'chosen one'. "The Chosen One, from our research through the inscriptions of an ancient language, is the one whose blood aligns with the ancestor."

The ancestor referred to here was known as 'Nife-en-Ank', meaning a breath of life translated from the ancient kemetic language from the oldest civilisation in Africa. He had an alias pet name his mother used to call him: Menelek, Rajesh pointed out to the duo.

So, Menelek was actually the crown prince, but his older cousins and younger brothers plotted to get rid of him so they could take over the kingdom. They were very envious of him and could not bear to see him take over. Since there was no possibility of killing him, they visited a very powerful oracle who, with immense witchcraft, managed to give him an early death. He was frozen inside the mirror but there was one catch he did not tell the brothers about. The price of such powerful magic was that his wealth and kingdom would be frozen too, until the rightful heir came along.

Menelek had a wife and two sons and a daughter. He loved his daughter so much and promised in his heart to bequeath her and her ancestral line the vast kingdom and wealth. When the deal was done, the envious brothers went ahead searching for the heirs of Menelek. When they reached their chambers, they discovered that Menelek's wife had run away with her children as they had been tipped off by a friend. They searched every town and city but could not find them. Menelek, inside the mirror, made sure that they could not be easily traced. The two boys grew older and married, while his daughter married a commoner and had five children with him.

CHAPTER FOUR

Menelek (Nife-en-Ank) and the Hidden Kingdom

Akana, after her parents' death, felt alone in this vast world. Every relative she knew turned cold and others would try to avoid her when they accidentally met in public places like the church or while commuting on public transport. These are the reasons why she stopped attending public gatherings of relatives. There were always those judging eyes and pity from others. There were these aunties patting her on the back and assuring her that she would find someone one day who would make her happy. Little did anyone know that there was an ancestral curse that had been working through the centuries and in her blood stream: the curse of Prince Menelek thousands of years ago. His descendants had gone through tough times, bad omens or short periods of leadership. There was something always opposing them preventing them from reaching their full potential. In this final chapter, Akana will put this bad omen to rest forever.

Rajesh told Akana to have a good night's rest, saying that the next morning, was when the real mission would begin. She slept through the night and in the morning, she was served a very hearty breakfast and some strange juice which Patel called brain juice.

"You need to drink a lot of that because your brain will be travelling through several centuries and time dimensions. Akana, you could get a chance to meet Menelek, your great ancestor!" Patel was very excited.

As exciting as it was, the process of travelling mentally into the past could be dangerous for Akana and possibly fatal. If her brain could not cope with the large amount of electrical current flowing through, then blood clots would start to form, leading to a stroke. All in all, there was the positive aspect that if her blood was of the right composition as she was the chosen one, then it would be a piece of cake.

Akana was directed to sit on a chair facing the mirror and her hands were strapped to the arms of the chair while one of the fingers was to be pricked by a thorn from the mirror so that a small sample of her blood would flow through it. Before anything commenced, Rajesh informed Akana that as she gazed through the mirror, she would probably drift through a slumber letting her mind travel back into the past, and cautioned her not to be distracted by anything but to recall her main mission: to meet Prince Menelek the ancestor.

"In case you get lost in the darkness or confusing pathways, follow the white monkey," he said in a shrill voice.

So Akana sat there waiting patiently, a little nervous and scared. As soon as one of the thorns pricked her finger, her body started fidgeting in the chair as if she was having seizures, then suddenly stopped as she drifted into a deep slumber.

Outside, Rajesh and Patel were anxious and thought that something was terribly wrong but suddenly there was a flash from the mirror, and the crack disappeared. The mirror looked as good as new and an image of Akana appeared, showing her walking along a pathway that branched forming numerous networks. She stopped and wandered around and a small white monkey appeared in one of the pathways and she followed it. Each pathway represented the blood lineage and white monkey was the spirit guide.

When she took the first turn following the monkey, she realised it was her mother's kinship and saw her mother with her family and siblings. Within seconds she saw herself getting younger so fast that she just became a tiny baby in her mother's arms, then disappeared into the womb. At the same time, all the places her mother had encountered as she was growing up became visible.

Rajesh and Patel could also see this through the mirror. Once Akana's mother disappeared into the womb, the monkey appeared on another branch of lineage pathway:

her grandfather's lineage, that is, the father of her mother. The process repeated itself through other lineages with the white monkey guiding her. In just five minutes, Akana managed to travel two centuries of her lineage, to the 1820s. There were no modern buildings, but typical African settlements, with rumors of European settlers coming in from Europe. Ten minutes went by, adding two more centuries, making it into the 1620s when the Muslim traders coming from the west as far as Morocco, moving into the Saharan desert in caravans.

Then the time in the mirror started passing as fast as lightning, until it slowed at the Middle Paleolithic Period, three hundred thousand years ago, during the emergence of modern humans, the Homo sapiens. The white monkey guiding Akana then disappeared. Almost an hour had gone by and Akana was still in deep slumber. There was a one-minute silence of no activity in the mirror and Rajesh thought that probably it was the end, or something had happened but before they could move or take any action, there was a flickering light as if from a burning wooden torch coming from the mirror.

A silhouette approached from the shadows, his face clear, looking at Rajesh very sternly and with confusion. His head was slightly enlarged. The closer he came to the mirror, the older he grew, with his hair turning grey, but his skin appeared as smooth as a baby's, and his complexion as dark as soot. He looked at Akana and called out her name twice and mumbled an ancient language which no one understood. Akana then opened her eyes slowly, looking ahead straight into the eyes of her ancestor. He began speaking to Akana in ancient language which Akana seemed to understand.

He said, "Akana, my daughter. It took you so long, but you came. Now there is no time to waste. I can feel danger looming ahead. The curse that my brothers put me in is now broken. I promised to bequeath you my kingdom and now it's all yours."

He extended his hand from the mirror and gave Akana a scroll. She took it and immediately Menelek disappeared into ashes.

The duo Patel and Rajesh unstrapped Akana from the seat and supported her by her arms, because the process she had gone through had weakened so that she could barely walk. She was advised to take a good meal and rest in order to regain her strength. Meanwhile, Rajesh would want to further examine the contents of the scroll and try to translate the ancient inscriptions. After sipping Patel's concoction of 'brain juice', Akana regained some energy and lay on her bed, her mind still fizzled and dizzy. She drifted into a deep sleep. Her subconscious led her to an ancient chamber like a study room of some sort. There she saw her ancestor Menelek drawing and jotting in an ancient language on a piece of canvas. He was using an ancient writing material. The room was filled with so many rolled up scrolls and ancient objects. The scrolls contained vast knowledge in science, agriculture, construction, technology, astrology, other realms and so many other aspects of life. In just entering the room, Akana could feel the flow of energy and the weight of the discoveries: so much unknown knowledge and phenomena that had been hidden because of the curse. She could see and feel her ancestor's encounters with a peculiar being.

Everything was jumbled in her brain. She then saw herself moving into another room, this time it was not made of stone or bricks; it was an open space. It felt as if she was standing on a cloud and she could feel the light breeze as she looked down to the ground so far below, with a few bird-like creatures flying by. Then Menelek extended his arm to Akana and directed her to sit on a throne-like golden chair suspended in midair in the clouds.

"I had the duty and responsibility of guardianship of Earth, guarding it from enemies and catastrophes. This responsibility is now yours. Do not be hesitant. I will always be there in case of anything," he spoke in ancient language.

All of a sudden there was a flash of light and Akana jerked from her sleep. She was sweating profusely, and her sheets were soaked in her sweat. She went to the bathroom and gazed at her reflection in the mirror. Nothing had changed, she was still the natural beauty she knew. Whatever Akana was experiencing now, due to her encounter with her ancestor, was part of her metamorphosis. Her brain was gradually growing with knowledge and wisdom, her cerebral capacity ever so slightly increasing, unlocking parts of her brain and abilities that were more than that of a normal human being. She was about to journey into a new world, with new responsibilities defining her destiny.

Rajesh had spent most of his adulthood collecting peculiar artifacts, encountering archeologists and now had become a member of Decagon Illusion. He had come across Menelek's story through ancient scribes and ancient languages and was immediately intrigued. He researched in detail and discovered a connection between Menelek and Homo sapiens species.

The Decagon Illusion's main aim was to oversee global issues and catastrophes, finding solutions to curb them. So they came up with a team of global representatives, hiring specialists such as archeologists, professors, meteorologists, doctors and many other professions. It was the group of archeologists and genealogists that came up with the theory of the Alpha 4.0 who contains the next humanoid species gene and whose DNA is the key to whole new worlds yet to be discovered. Menelek's story was central to their research. It was a longshot but they were positive of the results after many years of tests, trials and failures, they were not willing to give up. So Akana became the piece of the puzzle they had all been hoping for. So far, so good. They managed to access the mirror, breaking the curse where Menelek was imprisoned and obtained the scroll which probably was the next piece of the puzzle.

Akana proceeded to work closely with Mr. Rajesh to interpret the ancient maps and scrolls in search of the hidden kingdom that she had been bequeathed by her ancestor. Everything was easy for Akana since her encounter with Menelek. She could interpret the ancient languages and now had great knowledge of most disciplines because information seemed to be cascading from her brain with ease. Her ancestor also guided her in her dreams. After at least a month of research and use of the special compass they were able to produce the rough location of the hidden kingdom. The scroll handed over by Menelek to Akana, was written in parables but they were able to crack the code.

It was after this, that a general meeting was called of some members of the Decagon Illusion, leaving out the compromised ones, who assembled at the mansion in India. The President of the Republic of Kush and other presidents and prominent members of the society were present. Akana was privileged to meet them and most of the members were so eager and delighted to greet her and chat with her. The richest man in the world, James Francis Kulligan, often referred to by his initials J.F.K, took a photo with her and gave her his personal number and was mumbling about his latest project he was working on with artificial intelligence, robots and microchips. She had a great many proposals but was only focused by then on her current mission.

The head of Decagon Illusion introduced their mission, the latest discovery: Alpha 4.0 and her now acquired immense knowledge and capabilities. Rajesh then made his presentation on the new discoveries that there was indeed a hidden kingdom, and its location according to the coordinates on the special compass was a tiny island in the Indian Ocean. There was a catch, though. The kingdom was not actually on the island, but the island contained the entrance to the kingdom. Everyone in the room was confused and whispering. He then clarified that the scroll that was given to Akana by her ancestor was the key. The Chosen One was to hold up the scroll at a certain position facing the sun in the heart of the island and a door would appear. In other words, a portal. The portal would lead to a new world and time dimension in the further past.

During the time of Menelek, the kings were so powerful that they had enormous wealth and held supernatural responsibilities and positions. They had access to time portals that would enter different time zones. Menelek's father had a time portal that led further into the past where he established a hidden kingdom with all the wealth in the world. Back then, the world was just one huge super continent known as the Pangea. Since Menelek was the crown prince he inherited this kingdom and all the responsibilities of his father after he passed on. Five years into his reign he was cursed by his brothers and imprisoned in the magic mirror. The air molecules and flora and fauna in this new world might not be suitable for the modern-day man. So there should be a lot of training and preparations to be done for anyone to be ready to journey to this world.

Rajesh then ended his presentation by pointing out that such a journey would require thorough physical preparations and a budget to purchase the right equipment and devices. There was need for at least six months' training in simulations or low gravity areas. By the end of the meeting most members were fascinated by the idea of a new world. There could be animal and plant matter that could be studied and used to cure various diseases. A whole new world for scientists to explore and test specimens. All the members were then ushered into the dining hall for a lunch break.

Mr. James Francis, however, could not seem to take his attention from Akana. He was holding her hand and inviting her to sit at his table. If one could be looking at them from afar, one might think that he was attracted to her. And why not? Slim, with dark ebony skin and a young innocent face, Akana was indeed beautiful. James Francis had been married and divorced at least five times and he was about to turn fifty. Two of his ex-wives had children with him but the other three were super models and a socialite he had met at a club. Socially, he preferred to be the hunter looking for women and liked to dominate the courtship. So, when he saw Akana's rare beauty, he immediately followed his basic instincts. One more thing that made Akana stand out from his usual choice of women was her intelligence. He was charming her at the table showering her with compliments and talking about his travels and encounters all over the world, hoping to draw Akana's attention.

He said charismatically, "Do you know why they call you Alpha 4.0? You know alpha is a Latin word meaning first and 4.0 is the next humanoid species which is unnamed yet. The first, of course, being the Homo habilis followed by the Homo erectus and Homo sapiens and fourthly you, the mysterious Akana." Akana smiled and had nothing to say in response.

J.F.K whispered into her ear that he and Rajesh were old acquaintances and both enjoyed collecting mysterious objects. In fact, he had helped build and fashion the current mansion they were in. As they were chatting, Akana looked up and Rajesh and Patel were frowning across at their table. Rajesh was very uneasy, his eyes fixed at Akana as if to say *be careful of that slithering snake.*

After the lunch break, Rajesh approached Akana's table wearing a plastic smile on his face and casually greeted J.F.K who insisted that he needed a hug since they were old pals. As they patted each other's backs, Rajesh whispered into J.F.K's ear that he wanted to see him in the lobby. J.F.K was tall and well-built since he spent time at the gym and eating healthily to keep an attractive body. Surely, his attire, cologne and handsome face showed that he was a ladies' man.

They moved into the lobby holding hands and once they were out of everyone's sight, Rajesh stared at J.F.K sternly and said, "Look here, friend. Akana is not the type of girl for your love schemes. She is a very important asset for the mission and she needs no distractions until we uncover the hidden kingdom and so many other unknown phenomena. Any uncouth behavior on your side shall force you to be kicked out of the team."

J.F.K listened keenly and chuckled lightly. "Rajesh, Rajesh, Rajesh I am not trying to lure her into my bed, although she qualifies for that. Hey, just like the rest of you, I am intrigued by her intelligence and hoping I can get some insights for my latest projects tapping into some of her ancestral knowledge." He gave Rajesh a sly smile and went on, "After all, I came up with the genius idea of the cloning device in order to bring the 'endangered species' here safely, otherwise you would not have had anything to talk about today."

Rajesh responded by saying that it took an all-team effort to complete the mission of retrieving the Alpha 4.0 and plus he was paid handsomely for his device and any contributions.

J.F.K did not like where the conversation was heading, so he tried stirring it up a little. "We are buddies and we share some history together so we cannot let such small disagreements break our strong bond. I apologise if I offended you in any way. So, I will check my behavior around the asset," he stopped, trying to calm his friend down. It seemed to be working since Rajesh's tightened brow started loosening. J.F.K reached into his pocket and gave Rajesh one cigar, lighting it up for him.

As they shared a quiet moment smoking on one of the balconies, J.F.K revealed to his friend some information. "You see, my team stumbled upon something hidden in the World's Treasury's Charter. There are some articles providing for the "hidden kingdom" and member countries have been paying for it for many years in the form of taxes and referring to it as a last cause. There could be millions of dollars or even more belonging to this kingdom and Akana could stand a chance of inheriting this large estate and a huge bank account."

His eyes widened as he looked at his friend. Rajesh at first thought it was a joke and wanted to laugh out loud but J.F.K assured his old buddy to look into the World's Treasury's Charter in his own time. The rest of the day went smoothly as Akana retired to her room and most of the guests had left on their private planes to their respective countries.

Rajesh could not sleep that night. As he was on his bed in his room, he pulled out his tablet and googled the World's Treasury's Charter, carefully scanning through the Articles. There, under Article twenty-five, there were three clauses under the title 'last cause'. There was the first Article defining the last cause as an operation to be carried out in case of any imminent world danger or calamity such as a pandemic and natural disaster. The second Article dictated that it was incumbent for all member countries of the World Treasury to pay annual tax to the last cause account which could be accessed in accordance with the first clause. The third one read: *"Notwithstanding clauses one and two, the Last Cause Account can only be accessed by the rightful successor of the Bank of Sumeria."* There was no other definition of the successor of the Bank of Sumeria but in the interpretation of terms, right at the beginning of the Charter, Sumeria was defined as the oldest civilisation ever to have existed in Mesopotamia. Rajesh could not believe that such a clause existed right under their noses. Anyway, he still did not have enough information so he contacted the Head of the Decagon Illusion on that matter. He shared with him his findings, and he in turn contacted the President of the World Treasury, the global financial institution. World Treasury officials went through a thorough investigation on the locations and history of this Bank of Sumeria.

After two weeks Rajesh received a call from the Head of Decagon Illusion and they had an emergency video conference with the other members of the alliance. It turned out that the Bank of Sumeria might have originated in ancient Egypt and was transferred during the many conquests during the time of kingdom and emperors.

"It is the oldest account ever to have existed in the

World's Treasury," said the President of the World Treasury, "and it's still existing and now located in France and has been running all this time. The only problem is no one has ever accessed it to even find out how much is in it. It has some strange inscriptions."

The other members were astonished at these findings and though it was a long shot, they made a conclusion that it could be from the hidden kingdom from the time of Menelek. So therefore, Rajesh was tasked with the duty of travelling with Akana to Lyon in France, where the Bank of Sumeria is located in one of the largest banks.

So the following week Rajesh and Akana set course for France and only when they reached Lyon did the Head of Decagon Illusion contact them, directing them to meet up with one of the officials at the bank.

It was on a Saturday morning, that Rajesh and Akana approached the bank. The bank management chose that particular day in order to avoid prying eyes or in case anything went wrong. Akana was a bundle of nerves as she could not imagine how the experience would be. Would it be like the mirror incident? She had no idea. They followed the manager up the stairs and into a room. It was empty except for waiting chairs and a safe in the middle. Akana sat on one of the chairs and the safe was opened by the bank manager who entered a password. Inside the safe was a small device with a space on the side where you insert your finger for the fingerprint analysis. On the top of the device there was an ancient inscription which Akana was able to read. She translated it to the bank manager and Rajesh. It said *from Yeudomonia to Sumeria*.

"So that's what it means. All I see are just symbols and drawings," said the bank manager with a deep French accent.

"Yuedomonia is actually Menelek's kingdom; my ancestor," said Akana as if she was unsure of herself. She could not believe the words coming out of her mouth and how easily she could read and comprehend an ancient language that used symbols.

She took a deep breath and inserted her finger in the fingerprint reader on the machine. She felt a sharp prick but the machine would not release her finger yet. Then after one minute there was a click and it let go. Her finger was bleeding slightly and it felt as if it had been pricked by tiny needles. The bank manager handed her a tissue to wipe her bleeding finger and said how peculiar it was that the fingerprint reader had pricked her finger. Two minutes after the machine clicked, the screen on top of it started displaying numbers. It looked like a meter running numbers extremely fast, before halting at a figure.

Rajesh's and the bank manager's eyes widened as they saw the figure. It was a whopping fifteen trillion dollars. This was why the machine itself was referred to as the Bank of Sumeria. It was a treasury itself. The Sumerian emperor that acquired it from the conquest of an old kingdom in

Egypt. It could not be opened until it received a successor's blood. There had been several modern attempts to break the code by the French Bank. All this wealth now belonged to Akana: enough to run an entire kingdom for years. She was now the wealthiest woman in the world.

They both left France and returned to India. When they reached the mansion, word had already reached the Decagon Illusion of Akana's newly acquired wealth and everyone was in a celebratory mood. It was then that Akana received a phone call from her president who was already jubilating in the background.

"We are so proud of you, daughter of Kush. Congratulations!"

J.F.K was the first to arrive at the mansion aboard his private jet from America. He hugged Rajesh and Patel with a huge smile on his face. When he saw Akana he could not help but lift her up by her waist and congratulate her, referring to her as Her Majesty.

"This is a wonderful day! In fact, it's my birthday. I am turning fifty and you are all invited." He looked at Rajesh who was in mid-jubilation sipping a glass of champagne they had just popped to celebrate. Rajesh was not sure what J.F.K was referring to but then he insisted that they should all go on his private jet to America as special guests for his birthday. He was reluctant, but J.F.K went ahead to call the Head of the Decagon Illusion and other members to ask permission to travel with Akana, Rajesh and Patel to America for his birthday in his private jet. He pleaded with them that it would only take two days and he would bring them back as soon as possible.

After some thirty minutes contemplating on the matter the Decagon Illusion accepted on condition that Rajesh should pay close attention to Akana and should move with at least two bodyguards carrying the cloning device and a pistol. Rajesh was very unsure about this, but it was already happening so he boarded J.F.K's private jet hoping that the party would be over soon and they would be back at the mansion.

Their flight took almost two hours and they reached J.F.K's luxury home at eleven pm. It was massive, with a central swimming pool, enormous cascading chandeliers and amazing decor and furniture, indoors and out. It felt like a place of royalty. The guests had already arrived poolside and soothing music played from the speakers. Akana and her people were ushered into another room and Akana was advised to follow a female stylist who was going to help her change into a glamourous outfit and of course do her make up.

Rajesh pulled J.F.K aside and mumbled, "No funny business, eh. If you try to have carnal knowledge with her I'll report you to the team and you will be kicked out in no time. Patel here will follow her to the changing room and one of the bodyguards."

J.F.K had no choice but to accept. He could not believe how his friend could not trust him, but he knew he was acting like a father figure to Akana.

Several celebrities and dignitaries had been invited to J.F.K's birthday party. Akana could not ordinarily have attended such a party so it felt like a dream to her. She emerged from the changing room wearing a red designer gown and a long luxurious wig, the hair reaching below her waist, covering the open back of the dress. A pair of black elbow-length lacy gloves and black heels completed her chic look. J.F.K was amazed at how make up and attire could complete Akana's glamorous look. He instantly fell head over heels for her. He escorted her to the rest of the gathering, amid many stares and whispers. She knew that all attention was on her. The birthday boy did not look bad himself, in his white tuxedo. They crossed the red carpet to their table and he pulled out a chair for Akana. He was quite the gentleman that evening. Honestly, he had never felt so proud to be around a woman for years. He had pure admiration for Akana and tried very much to please her.

The night went on until the cake was cut and toasts were made. Then the dance music began. J.F.K wished to dance with Akana on the dance floor but Rajesh strongly opposed. Rajesh was seated at the same table with them, and Patel at the other end. Patel was busy on his phone and was not even bothered by the party. People were streaming in to greet J.F.K and wish him well on his birthday, and others could not resist asking who his lady escort was. Rajesh would quickly say she was just a friend but J.F.K told one or two guests that night that she was a princess from Yeudomonia, a very ancient Kingdom.

Rajesh was feeling uneasy and anxious for the party to end because he had a strong feeling that something fishy was going on. However, when J.F.K was called by one of his employees over some urgent issue and left the table, Rajesh saw an opportunity to have a quick cigarette to curb his nicotine urge. He instructed Patel to stay close to Akana and make sure she did not leave the table. The other two bodyguards were nearby watching. The waiter brought in a fresh tray of wine glasses and Akana picked one from the tray and so did Patel. As the waiter was leaving, Akana noticed that one of her earrings was missing so she bent over at the table to reach for it. When she sat up again after failing to find her earing, Patel was smiling at her nervously. She took a sip at her glass and two other sips before J.F.K suddenly appeared, pulling her from the table for a dance, since he could not see Rajesh.

Two minutes into the dance, Akana started complaining to J.F.K that she was feeling dizzy. As her head was reeling and spinning so fast, she asked J.F.K to take her back to the table but before they reached it, she collapsed into his arms and fell on the floor. There was a commotion around her as she was drooling while white foam came out of her mouth.

From the corner of her eye she could see and hear Patel on the phone saying, "Yes, Master. It is done. Now is the time …"

She could not hear any more, because a woman let out a blood-curdling scream. Rajesh, upon hearing this, rushed back only to find Akana's body lying unconscious.

www.ingramcontent.com/pod-product-compliance
Lightning Source LLC
Chambersburg PA
CBHW011522070526
44585CB00022B/2507